NOTES
FROM THE COUNTRIES
OF BLOOD-RED FLOWERS

MACDARA WOODS

Dublin

DEDALUS

The Dedalus Press
24 The Heath,
Cypress Downs,
Dublin 6W
Ireland

Acknowledgements : some of these poems have appeared in
*Cyphers, The Poetry Ireland Review, The Irish Times, Dedalus
Irish Poets, The Kilkenny Anthology, Thistledown (Poems for
UNICEF)* and *Toward Harmony*.
The author is grateful to the family of Heinrich Böll for time
spent in the Böll cottage on Achill Island, and to Bernard and
Mary Loughlin and to all the staff at the Tyrone Guthrie Centre
at Annaghmakerrig, where many of these poems were written.
He is grateful, too, to the Irish Writers' Centre, the Cultural
Section of the Department of Foreign Affairs and to the Maxim
Gorki Literary Institute, Moscow, for a visit to Russia. Thanks
to Nikolai Krassikov and Winfried Scheidges for their great
personal kindness there, and to Paul Cahill and Nando Trilli for
friendship, and a glimpse of Prospero's Garden in Umbria.

ISBN 1 873790 44 9 (paper)
ISBN 1 873790 45 7 (bound)

Cover design by Matthew Blake

Dedalus Press Books are represented and distributed abroad by
Password, 23 New Mount St., Manchester M4 4DE.

The Dedalus Press receives financial assistance from An
Chomhairle Ealaíon, The Arts Council, Ireland.

In memory everything seems to happen to music. That
explains the fiddle in the wings.
Tennessee Williams: "The Glass Menagerie".

If I were Rimbaud I wouldn't need the music.
Serge Gainsbourgh

Poetry is religion, religion without the hope.
Jean Cocteau

I dream of poems like the bread-knife
Which cuts three slices at once
Hugh MacDiarmid

If you cannot – in the long run – tell everyone what you have
been doing, your doing has been worthless.
Erwin Schrödinger

Everything I earned and learned has gone with the tap of a
spoon against the teeth.
Milorad Pavić

For Niall –
who reminds me

CONTENTS

Distances

Blues Note For John Jordan   33

Distance And Line

La Befana Bearing Gifts   53

Notes From The Margin

Notes From The Countries

DISTANCES

LES CÔTES DU TENNESSEE

The colours you will walk in little son
these countries that are yours were mine
were magical and strange such contradictions
the space bat angel spread its wings
and came down burning from the sun –
are magical and strange and dangerous
and oh the world is full of crooks and heroes
beware the cargo when your ship comes in
the autumn serpent in the stubble field
those patient spiders in our dusty rooms
have registered and taken note
and hold us in their thousand eyes

Forty one years later the tune still plays
through this April afternoon my birthday
in the skies above the Lost River Ranch
Highway 76 and the Mississippi delta
Les Côtes du Tennessee and *Beausoleil*
the space bat dragon loops and sings
make me an angel that flies from Montgomery
send me a poster of an old rodeo
just give me one thing that I can hold on to
and the world is full of crooks and heroes –
I have been listening since East Liberty
since West Palm Beach and since the dawn

Vrai Citoyen du Monde like Thomas Paine
of all the dawns alone or shared in empty rooms
or standing by a ship's rail watching
this self-same Mississippi sun come up
down East of Wexford and the Tuskar Rock
in flight from time and circumstance – at
thirty thousand feet above pretence we start
to drop for Arkansas and South Missouri
new rooms new names new answers friends
as the space bat angel dragon sings
in a world made right for crooks and heroes
that if defeated we fly down in flames

9

STATION PLATFORM: SANDYMOUNT

At 48 stoop-shouldered come to rest
and grief I say that's it enough
I quit on grief in action and on all of it
disentangled from the truth
such fantasies need time and life
and too much time and life of late –
I'll quit this city and these burning shapes
of smuts and ashes on the wind
smoking and smouldering those neon lights
the snipers under greasy eaves
birds of prey on the bedroom wall
and love in caves beneath the streets

I will find out where this river goes
before it meets the sea – and to deserve
all proffered friendship and affection
I'll salute old friends lost friends
old afternoons from all of twenty years ago
unfold a half-forgotten yellow map
to walk Boródino a while unharmed –
the lock gate opens on the Marne canal
and slow green water spills out over
all the afternoon in Moncour – Niall and I
are walking side by side this dry July
following the international barges

To see what happens what occurs
behind the trees and round the bend – we come
upon my father skimming stones
these ten years dead and skimming stones
my sabbath father on the shore
alone and dark at Sandymount

by the railway track and the cold sea-baths
come back a black-eyed exorcist
waiting silent where the river goes
before it meets the sea
before we parted company – Can you recall
alive refashion this his black eyes ask?

Look Dad Look – says Niall this afternoon
in Moncour and cocks a whiplash arm –
This is how your father skimmed a stone

BLOOD-RED FLOWERS

I thought it was another country
and I find it is
another country of the blood-red flowers
here in your rainswept house
Semitic characters in chalk
still linger on the gate-post
not washed away by the wind and rain –
through the same distorting lens
of leaded glass I see
mad creatures climb the garden wall

And finding out again again
that no one constitutes a harbour
just another afternoon of rain
and turning round and round
in an inflammatory circle – so
to pick up all the pieces now
whose job is that? To sort
through all this durable detritus
these weary sentences
those unfinished bits of glass

With no names engraved thereon
that's it? I should have given up
on it? Long since? You think?
Kept one eye always on the clock and left
before the neon lights came on
been ready to accept the gifts
of emptiness and avocado stones
and then put on my hat and coat
to follow the French accordeon
out again past the edge of town

Should have done but didn't
not even when the set collapsed
and the rustic roof fell in
in a shower of Tarot cards
with the balcony in bits I was
still the stroller on the boulevard
lost in that El Paso game of dice
looking for a way into your space
with no words left to say
still spinning to the end of play

And yet for us I never doubted
but that we are kindred in the skin
with all the same desires regrets
we can put on take off the secret parts
like gloves – in the park today
three figures called me in the rain
to join them in a shadow game
of moving on to answer
to the whisper on the 'phone –
I need to make you want to
come to me you'll come

THE BANKS OF THE DANUBE

(after the Dordán concert in Butler House, Kilkenny, January 1991)

In another City nearly fifty
and that slow air tears my lungs
ageing backlit figure
in the shadows out of focus
some dark night outside
and time stops still – I am
the floating isolated skull
over there in the smoky corner
the faded picture on the poster
fallen down behind the till
still looking out for love

Cold and listening to music
slow air and punctured lungs
plans shelved again and
folded up in Rand McNally
that woman in Chicago
who slept with a loaded gun –
have I somehow outlived them all
the lovers and the drunks
and all my dispossessed
my own poor lost hussars at one
with moonlight and blue music

Music in the air tonight
that slow air tears my lungs
and women comb the killing fields
to find dead lovers news of men
stretched naked in the streets
so cold so white as ice tonight
beneath the Precinct wall
along the levee and the slips
on the river-walks and quays
by this salt fatal river –
this landlocked frozen sea

Trapped until Winter cracks
in the ice outside your door
tomorrow morning I will ask –
St Brigid's Day the first of Spring –
which road to take to catch
my nineteen-forties distant self
walking in unfamiliar snow
the sting of sea foam in my mouth
rock salt in the fields – tonight
this same slow air is yours
this slow air fills the room

ANOTHER APRIL: FATHER HAYDEN BOSHEEN

for Margaret Cosgrave

On the foot of your kind welcome back
I am walking in to the City happy
thankful and glad for Eve and the apple
at ease in Kilkenny in the evening sun
and pausing in St Patrick's Churchyard
mindful of times drinking wine by the neck
in graveyards or smoking long cigarettes
in graveyards or devouring Hoffman-LaRoche
until I become as invisible
as the children I hear at play – as unseen
as the bird that rustles in the tree above me
now all our names are weathered from the stones
and – as indication I am not a vampire
my shadow cast by the setting sun

WALKING FROM GRAIGUE: May 1991

I'd say we escaped from gravity
even if only for half a day –
somewhere on the train between
John's Quay and Stephen's Green
by Muine Bheag and Carlow
Athy Kildare – or Dunmore Cave
on tiptoe on the dizzy steps

Or down the river bank
in May from Graiguenamanagh
walking to St Mullins Churchyard
five miles along the Barrow
for no single reason other
than the simple beat of promise
pulsing in the heat of summer

To be found innocent at last
and doing the best we can
though it is too late now perhaps
at noon to lie down in the sun
with no past history no
narrative save water – such summer
innocence is at a premium

Like all the sunlit countryside
its weight and history
the rituals of blood and tides
and time and birds – the unknown
image in the mirror in a room
where lovers lie awake at night
and think themselves alone

Is a but an image from the stones
near Moling's Churchyard
Norman motte outside the gate
the shadow of the vanished tower
on the grave of Bryan Na Stroake
and Bird-Man Sweeney still astray
amid the noise of crows

Killed by a jealous husband
hereabouts the story goes
did he too feel the urgent steps
upon the stairs that night
and did the woman with black hair
quaerens quem devoret drift
somehow into the portrait – at

Which another image comes to mind
my uncle and his cracked abuse
one day my sister faced him down
The Spanish Bitch The Spanish Bitch
astride a hill in Co Meath
deranged by passion over land
his white hair whipping wind

And in this present country now
this place of jumping Saints
and diving cormorants
a second – other – woman with black hair
comes back to me unclear
a memory half-captured once at night
a face behind a fall of oranges

Behind a footfall on the stairs
though she was French I thought
remembering the portrait
the broken glasses and the guns
the voices raised the sound
of tables overturned – but maybe
as before I have it wrong

At odds pursuing images
between the trees I seem to see
again the judge's son passed out
upon the Courthouse steps
the morning of Assizes – his
covenant he knew not cod
but better to believe we do

If everything is fiction
or mere licensed fantasy – and yet
these times I'm walking through
my figures in the stream
of cormorants and Suibhne Geilt
or one red squirrel in a tree
answering-back another May

Do not themselves turn meaningless
or metamorphosed out of true
become a catalogue of figments –
the histories unfolding here
are no less sinister – I do not see
this day in time grow any less
insistent real or dangerous

But then none of this is fantasy –
and truth is less cosmetic
than the fictions of self-publicists
or those who work to make it to the Papers
as in *"Eoghan Harris Lashes*
Media in Twink Furore" – such
public flagellation of caprice

Or how to hype the system up
to orchestrate the news in terms
of two-inch furies – screaming
front-page headlines on the day
five million public pounds went lost
and Goodman Enterprises Inc
moved smoothly into Ballybay

Until at last we half believe
it has become unreal to take
a brief time-off from craziness
unshadowed by the face of bathos
painted on a big balloon
somehow to block that cartoon voice
of broadcast public conscience

The deadly daily grit inside our skulls –
wondering can we hold our peace
fighting every mortal step
to keep an ordinary faith intact –
austere – with memory as metaphor
aware we can't withdraw too much
for fear we lose our common touch

And this too is history to walk
the high-wire of the river stretched
from lock to grey-stone lock
not withered up or opting out
just walking through the present
almanac of being alive reliving
the politics of all our summers

And in the end I'll stay here
– for the moment – with this stream
of memories and maddened men
the shadow of the tower no more
the black-haired woman in the portrait
an opaque spider on a stem
for ever *quaerens quem devoret*

DISTANCES: SOUTH MISSOURI NOVEMBER 1991

for Kathryn Buckstaff

Glimpsed from a Greyhound Bus
the eighteen-wheeler reads
Grief Brothers on the highway
and we're pitching down
Interstate 44 from St Louis
in the snow – driven
by a Born Again Christian
whose Night Rider eyes contain
the certainty of resurrection
beyond tomorrow and the bill-boards

Tonight I read-off history
reading off the magic names
racketing past the Meramec Caverns
Six Flags Over Mid-America
Eureka Bourbon Cuba
Sullivan and Lebanon
Waynesville and Fort Leonard Wood
all Legend and the Legend is
Explanation of Symbols
or *How To Determine Distance*

Tomorrow or the next day
you will take me to a hidden place
of upland silences – the road
leads down into the lake
and we move off into the winter hills
to eat persimmons and black walnuts
looking south to Arkansas: in
recognition I salute these places –
say their names: *Manor Kilbride*
Moon City – Hollister
and *Poulaphuca Lacken* Branson

DISTANCE AND FUNERAL: MEATH DECEMBER 1991

1.

The people here prehistory
who carved these stones
what messages and how to read them

Are only voices in the wind
the sound of rooks and daws
crow-sounds in winter

Are also all my childhood
the darkness and the dripping trees
grow brown and all around

Corroding mortar flakes
pieces slither from the walls
to crumble in the winter grass

2.

I am no longer part of this
but was I ever – did I ever fit
into my memory of how it was

Or is the restless movement all
returning home on spinning wheels
going back for funerals

Becoming part of life
half-way through unfinished stories
and called away before the end

3.

And yet – what messages
must be there in the genes what
blueprints from the distant people

The solar masons who
built permanence along the Boyne
and vanished into wind and rain

As you did too my Famine
ancestor – my travelling man from Cavan
who came here on a load of eels

And stopped and stayed and showed
us other passage graves to read
and other histories to learn

I feel the same repeated touch
of hoarseness in my voice – that tell-tale
change of pace along the road.

TIME OUT

Rooks are feeding in the sloping field
between us and the sea
two twin dark birds – and here
remains of last night's fire and fishbones
are all the messages we leave –
again another night and we
have tidied up and cleared away the traces

Returning mid-December on a sunlit day
through fields of winter cattle
their damp hides steaming
I asked could you live somewhere else
expecting your reply might come
from music – our damp history
and the music maker's ruined lungs

Straining in smoky kitchens:
that history we never learned
as such but share – this country of denial
where we are of the landscape where we are –
travelling back unknown
together from the ocean inlet
to the towns locked in by windows

And beyond the windows rooms
where lovers talk and touch
till all the world is minuscule –
the truth behind the lessons learned
along the railway tracks: that
certainties provide no refuge – that
nothing lasts but the desire

Taking this same knowledge back
crushed into a window-frame
I look down from the train and know
that there will always be
uncertain figures on the further shore
beyond the two black birds that feed
between us and the sea

INTERIOR: THE GREAT FISH

What fails me then to get to this
so empty – empty as an egg-shell in the grass –
but May again triumphalist?
Laburnum lilac chestnuts dust
the gutters of the sunlit road
another year has come and gone
and Niall just turned nine
he tells me now is feeling almost ten:
fearful for the human heart
I try to put a gloss on this

And think of Dr Hook and Lucy Jordan
who'll never ride through Paris with
the warm wind in her hair –
this time in Paris last year
half-translated I sat down to make a note
in sunlight in the Rue Berzelius –
no bad thing either
to stop alone at some oasis –
holding a virgin telecarte
still hooked-up to the Universe

It's not enough but it may do
in time to put an edge on things
to find a way back in
without traduction – swamp creatures once
we now come down to water here
between the trees beside this pool
and make display of well-oiled parts:
among the bones and tracks of dinosaurs
we too can leave
the marks of marvellous birds

BORROWED DAYS

Last year in Limerick
in a poet's house
I watched two cats
fly past the window
I have not been here
long enough:
evening comes

A mad dog leaped
to catch me by the throat
three weeks ago
in Dublin
missed and
tore my clothes:
the day approaches

From behind a bar
in Mayo
just last week
a dog attacked
and bit me in the knee:
time passes unprovoked
the day comes closer

This side of
the country of the fish
we've been astray
no explanation
but out on the bog at night
the moon
stone boats

FIDELITIES

Darkness initially and then
the same soft under-water focus
drifting weeds
a sea-cave lit by candles
and failing yet again to make a contact
once more I put the question
from twenty years before

What do you think of?
What goes on in there?

Nothing – she smiles –
nothing whatever: inside here
there is emptiness
all this is emptiness

In sudden neon lighting
she reconstructs a face

An emptiness of such complexity
that I am lost if I begin to think
and if that is what she chooses
to present
this enigmatic porcelain
who am I to disbelieve –
bring down upon my neck
some less acceptable dimension
of man or bird
yet another fall to earth
or any killing of your choice

Perhaps the pheasant
in the clothes-shop window?

It was in a mirror that I saw
so long ago so long ago
that intermittent flash of red
those flames that dance and lift –
the shower of sparks
on limbs that shift and fall
like logs on burning embers

BLUES NOTE
FOR JOHN JORDAN

A bird was in the room.
– Franz Kafka

BLUES NOTE FOR JOHN JORDAN
FROM ST JAMES'S HOSPITAL JUNE 1992

Dear John – I miss you greatly
in pain and doped
last night in the William Wilde Ward
after surgery I slept
and dreamt of you
cruising Ireland in an open car
some timeless Summer in the 1950s
surrounded by friends and phantoms
with hampers bottles books
or sitting on a lawn recounting
stories without rancour
before you all moved on to view
the grey stone house in the meadow
lion and shells above the lintel
with no intention there of horror
haemorrage or shadow –
but time enough to think of that
when you come walking home from Santiago

I woke at six and all around
in daylight white as salt-flats
angels and poets were waking up
in hospitals and houses
just like everybody else
kicking aloft their heels and skirts
coming-to alone with others
or losing themselves in sex
discreetly in the suburbs
or shambling solitary
from gaps along the city quays
and open spaces of the Fifteen Acres –
clients of the morning shake
in early bars and railway stations
spin-drift drinkers
sea-pool creatures stranded

Clutching votes for Maastricht
some run aground at Dollymount
and some rise up with flocks of birds
to track across to Booterstown
or settle into Dublin 4
marching across the marshes
like frog-princes to the dogs
some learn like you the code of cloisters
discipline in laid-out books
while others find their own escapes
making vows of abstinence
in meeting-rooms in Aungier Street –
and still the whirling city
floats in air
swaying waves of football crowds
come riding up the river Swan
from Shelbourne Road to Harold's Cross
new colonists from Bristol
quick-silver to the plimsol
sailing home on mercury
without the trick of Cocteau's gloves –
and *Orpheus Lives* in Effra Road

The room was bright with light
when I came back
post operative and slightly crazed
my life before my eyes
in shock half-naked lurching
from my bed to walk
St James's corridors alone
premonitory gathererer at fifty
flapping and hopping from crack
to crack – a solitary dancer
picking up my bits of bone
from furnaces and city dumps
split images and sleight of sound
dried streaks of blood
my broken bits of city speech –

In his last hours
the soldier with the bandaged head
heard voices from the street
à bas Guillaume à bas Guillaume
heard gulls and slogans
on the breeze – *à bas Guillaume*
and *I'm for Europe*
slogans voices
gulls' voices in the wind
and I'm for Europe too
God knows: we never left it John
wandering here for forty years
as it goes on
in all its endless contradictions –
the histories of Sarajevo
corpses at the gates of Moscow
churros at dawn among the dead
a sometime morning entertainment
on the roads around Madrid
the barbarous New Jerusalem
grown up across the water
status quo expedience
and that vindictive smiling
senile Master of The Rolls
Wehrmacht and Bundesbank
poison clouds above Kiev
Charlemagne and Stupor Mundi
the filthy bombing of Iraq
not the placard stuff of slogans
something to write home about
complacently –
remembering our own perspective
the only Post-Colonial
State in Western Europe –

remembering Dublin afternoons
upstairs rooms in empty colleges
dead souls dead unforgiven souls
and all the dusty shelves
with rows of cardboard boxes
full of human skulls and bones
and human stories – stolen
shameful catalogues
of other plundered peoples

There is a wind of politics
a wind that blows about our walls
not just our European history
Hitler and St Francis of Assisi –
for all that we may walk today
in Harold's Cross among laburnums,
from Sceilig Michíl to the Albaicín
do penance in Jerusalem
or make the journey from St Jacques
the pilgrim road to Santiago
with silver wings upon our heels
tomorrow in Bohemian Grove
or Berchtesgaden
or some other version of the Bunker
serious heads of state will sit
drinking from a human cup
without reflecting surfaces
Greek Fire or Pepper's Ghost
or the magician's smoky glass –
it will be real no artifice
no mime of tinsel there or heartbreak
but toasts to commerce and to murder
drinking to the dispossessed
whose unforgiving skulls they use
Ai Ai Hieronymo

And still we carry on
while there is sunlight in the corridor
the news ticks in piles up
from all points of the compass –
The winter will be hungry
and the hard winds blow

But none of this is news to you
old hand at hospitals
recidivist of love
highwire traveller at night
European tight-rope walker
attender at infirmaries
astonisher and puzzlement
old mentor *veterano* ВЕТЕРАН
in eight years more we're of an age
and never were too far apart
in eight years' time another date
another century at fifty-eight
a new millennium and gravitas
but you are gone and I must ask you this –
did St Theresa give a damn
for your discalcèd Indian?

DISTANCE AND LINE

Unless that's a scorpion and he was stuck there
for millions of years, and that's his shadow that stayed.
— Niall Woods

CLARE ISLAND: AUGUST 1992

What to say about this?
Nothing more than sitting
in this white sand
with my back to a rock
looking over at the Reek
stunned by the sun
on this melting clock-face
drowned in the sweep
of blue and meerschaum –

It is five o'clock
and I will not stand up
not travel any further
the sun has pinned
my cells against the light
and I will always be
this moment – a flash of
voices from the pier
those same two lovers framed
apart together
at the water's edge

And further out is
nothing more than this –
is nothing more than concave sea
a painted stationary boat
bow pointed East for Louisburg

NIGHT SOUNDS

This is what I do these marks upon a page
is what I do and all I do
and I am caught here fighting with it – fighting
with myself with interruptions and with silence
finding messages and wondering what's the use:
a wind that howls about the house
could bring me home
the stream that breaks its banks at night

Can bring me nowhere: the hunger that I need
escapes into the rotting leaves
beneath the walnut tree: spurious warmth of ash:
again I fear I have lost touch with language –
can answer only now to touch itself
and half-remembered images and music: did I not
go deep enough into that same morass
to bring back music? Bring you back?

Went back among the dead to tell it:
and found my father threatened by Hibiscus
drenched with whiskey howling in his sleep:
nightly wrestling with the moon – the moon
of Jacob's Ladder or the truth below:
downstairs the dreadful sisters taking root –
night visitors with surgeons' knives
rehearsing their persuasions for the wake –

Landscape and history: unhappiness does not
come into it – that's how it was
at best refusing to renegue on faith –
observing some appointed trust: at worst
not ripping tongues from rusty bells
living in the fire and not the flame
drinking slanted sunlight from the well
not falling to the bottom of the lake –

Tonight the distant lights are quiet:
moon and time have run aground – my household
here in sleep has worn away the circuits
thrown damp grass and salt upon the fire
and still it moves: just outside this house
my far out furthest planet from the Sun
new-born new-launched Galileos
drift unseen past the shutters of my room

SCHOOL BUS: VIA CIGNE

On my first day back from Russia
I walked down to the road to meet you
coming home on the school Pulmino

Glad to be home wherever home is
benign in the present hour of grace
I wave to the children on the bus

Well Dad – you say – that's all right too
but you know how it is
there can be enemies on the bus

And yes I understand how that can feel
when you begin to be convinced
either that you are somehow alien

Or that all the others on the bus
your fellow travellers themselves
have come from outer space

And not like MacBryde's Venusians –
so beautiful – he said – he couldn't tell
if they were girls or boys –

Sometimes it happens in the middle
of the night – when you discover
that there's no one else on the ship

Just you and the lights burning
the engine throbbing and those dark
patches in the corridors:

A blazing ship full of people passing
the Lizard at midnight
and there's no one there at all

THE THUGS AT THE DOOR OF THE INTOURIST HOTEL

The toughs at the door
of the Intourist Hotel
would keep out Chagall's white doves –
Natasha and Tania
who float above their heads
like summer birds –

Because they are not hip
or mafia or flash
not part of this – not selling
promises or flesh
but speak instead of poetry
of space
and distant clouds of silver birches

The thugs at the door
of the Intourist Hotel
will allow me to pass because
I am foreign
and better have dollars
to pay thirty times the price
for a cup of coffee

The thugs at the door
allow mainly gangsters in –
but nobody knows for sure
who the gangsters are
the thugs on the floor
the thugs on the door
or the thugs behind the bar

Only the hotel pianist
appears to have it right
he strips the tired
pink plastic drapes
from the once white instrument
sits down
and plays us Mack The Knife

ACORNS FROM PAVLOVSK

for Eugenia Alexandrovna Ravtovich

For so long and so often
it seems to be a race
against something:
trying to get back to the angel
before the fuel runs out –
Burning the wheel-house
in mid-Atlantic
or running against time
lungs hope or drink

Where are you
oh secret lovers?
We send out letters
no one answers
Where are you
Dead Fathers?
Where are you
oh railway stations?

Then somewhere on the journey
it all comes simpler:
a porcupine feather
two white snail-shells
in my garden
walnuts from the tree
in late October –
and in my pocket
these five acorns
I have carried from Pavlovsk

THE PARADISE SEXY SHOP

(A Note Of Thanks for Ciaran O Driscoll)

Driving from here to the city you will find
the Paradise Sexy Shop
just past the village of Strozzacapponi
not far from the Fairground
pick-up quarter – when the moon is right
lights glitter on the roundabout
and cars slow down pull up take off

Eiléan and Niall have gone to the fair
to celebrate the *Fiera dei Morti* –
tonight or tomorrow we'll be eating
fave dei morti with apples and nuts:
but for now my son is sailing in the *Barca*
Halloween is hanging from the rafters
and the ship flies up and up

In Peredelkino among the leaves
Lev Oshanon eighty – five times married
Soviet balladeer lover and poet
is putting the last fine cut
to his life and work: *A Half A Century
of Love Betrayal Jealousy* –
he dedicates it to his present wife

You should have come when you drank
he says – and gives us Volga carp and Vodka
apple-juice fire and welcome – two musicians
play the words: *when I think of all
the women who have loved me –
in that poisoned day
then I remember the woman I betrayed*

There is a filament that runs through this
the central nervous system of a fish –
I do not see the patterns in the fire
I see the fire itself and that's enough:
for we are human and we could be doing worse
than driving half across the world to find
the Paradise Sexy Shop

HILL-WALK: EPIPHANIA 1993

(for Natalia Georgievna Vasilkovskaya)

New morning resurrection
you could believe in that –
up here where the air is sharp
as cock-crow after Christmas
and the shooting stops

Almost believe in poetry
to take you back to where you were
now that other
difficult identities
have left the stage –
                    you could believe
in working here with words of ice
constructing sounds
and cutting figures out of space

As from a different angle
that chess-board house and trees
four-square Italian hill-demesne
is not dissimilar
to Planter Farms I knew in Meath

And that staccato sound just now
was it your heart you heard
drumming on the bar?
Bells ringing in the street outside –
that's also where you were

And at the latter end
there's few enough of us left
And that's the truth – Damn few Macdara
Myself and yourself is all
Only the pair of us in it

Only yourself and myself
walking from vacant room to room
ignoring the rattle in the corners –
sea creatures
that we share the house with –

Today the Feast of the Epiphany
yourself myself and Niall
are playing cowboys in the yard:
The earth gives praise –

Thank you thank you thank you
thank you Colle Calzolaro
thank you for the scattered houses
thank you thank you
birds and lizards
and thank you thank you thank you
for that Christmas card from Moscow

LA BEFANA BEARING GIFTS

Thus, if one just keeps on walking,
everything will be all right.
— Søren Kierkegaard

LA BEFANA BEARING GIFTS

My Dear –
at 50 there are problems other
than lying awake at night
listening to time
tick by – and maybe
I should get up go out
but it's early yet
to be walking abroad
through the morning fog
to be vexed by questions
besides our usual
right affairs of Lilliputians
cold and growth
whether the winter wood will last
and flies again in January

Still I put on my boots
in hope
that in the rhythm of the movement
on the road
or climbing up some forest path
I yet might separate
the players from the set
by accident –
discover how you can shut out
uneasy bird-cries
and the noises-off
the fury in the undergrowth –
or find a fragile skin
suspended from a bush
still raw still chill
dead remnant from
the years I lived outside
camped-out on window sills
nomad of the concrete paths
stalker of the concrete parks –

In-flight that
tape-worm reel unfolds
inside my head again
and I remember
aquiescence and pretence
suspect act of faith
first believing in the script
and then believing I believed
my misplaced trust in
Sammy Glick repeated
good notices I wrote
for Captains Young and Winsome
Captain Sammy Glick
and Captain Cod

       But now
forgetting for a moment
such mistakes
forgetting Sammy Glick in operation
the daily farce of
What Makes Sammy Run
mean truth of mean decision makers
and Great Anthologisers
doing the books
drowned in whiskey
settling scores
drunk beneath the eaves
of Georgian Squares
what I remember most
from all my spinning years
is being alone –
the emptiness of waiting
for the fitting words to come
of waiting catching maybe
an early glimpse
of Mrs Aeolus Carney

stiff-backed in a dressing-gown
scattering crumbs
from a bag of laundry
Juno in a city garden
hanging out the clothes
or Isadora Duncan
summoning the Russian winds –
not much not much
but picaresque enough
something that would work to keep
the watcher on his feet

       And
what should I have done
to change all this
but change all this and so I did?
Come in like a bird
from the weather?
Jerking from perch to perch
or hopping up
and down the steps
scratching on a table top
nodding cap and bells
against the glass?
Trailing a wing and beating
its beak against the glass?

Instead I just said stop
and gave up dying
gave up drink and gave up
dancing with the dead
came to and
took the image by the throat –
but when you find
that I and all the other
figures in the scene

have somehow become autonomous
as self-contained
as cattle in a field
you ask me what to do –
what should you do
to keep in place
the fragile curtains we
put up against the wind –
and I reply
that this wind cuts us both
from here on out
we must be careful
to look each and every gift-
horse in the snout

And last September
when the house was full of drunks
I worked at it
along the forest trails
around the countryside
I walked and thought
of cutting losses
cutting loose
remained polite
considered Separate Houses
all day and every day
the maundering talk
of food and drink repeated
drove me out
and I unable to escape
or move into another place
walked all the hills around
stayed out for days
in exile from myself and time
my household life and work
and left the drunks behind
to puppeteer at keeping house – but

how did it appear to you
and how was it for me?

We do not have to justify
the truth
of how we feel
nor yet apologise
for anger at being forced
to breathe sour air
nor make appeasing smiles
at noise and overcrowding –
when I drank
I lived with drunks and some of those
I loved the most
were drunks who spoke in poetry
who burned like fire
and conjured pictures
out of air
despite which I was thankful
when the gift-horse came
to dump me in the mad-house
thankful even
for the snake-pit
the indignity and pain
and no more *apologia*
and that was all so long ago –
I am not here today to play
at country life
or keeping country house –
just being here
and being here with you
to deal with fires and rooves
and all the making do
and patching up
that fills a year
and being here to think and work

to find my way around a book -
and in the end
good-will alone is not enough
I have good-will
but do not need
intrusion of this other kind
this tedium
of alcoholic sweat
and talk
without the poetry
without a glint of flame in it

And we no doubt shall find some
resolution
as we always do –
it will be transient
as all our resolutions are
the quick sharp joy
of something found
or something done
of meaning coming through –
a few days back I found
a frozen mirror in a hedge
unbroken silver skin
reflecting sky
a few weeks back
a dead bird in the grass
blue throat and ruffled wings
such winter gifts Befana brings
today the air is clean
and once again
the tractors
have begun to beat
the new-lit hills
and once again the field
between us and the road

is turning green
spun parallels of grain new-woven
run together like a twill
grass beneath the vines is gone
beans and garlic planted
bamboos cut – and
after wind and sun the lane
feels almost sandy underfoot
        the countryside
is moving into Spring

tomorrow maybe
we should start to build
that long-projected summer hut

Tavernelle di Panicale

NOTES FROM THE MARGIN

You ugly child. Show me your friends
and I will eat them.
The old blind man in "The Famished Road".
– Ben Okri

A MAP OF VALENTINE 1993

Yesterday on St Valentine's Day
all the birds of the townlands
chaffing in the trees
talking and choosing the season's mate
was also the Feast of the Cats
biding their time to speak
and seen from this end of the valley
improbable between the olives
Panicale loops like a Bristol Bridge
suspending its fret-saw stretch of sky
above the lake's reflected light

Città della Pieve to my left
in the mist – where the Sacristan
waits for unwary women –
adjacent Missiano sinks into the fields
astray behind me Tavernelle
and on my right skirts lifted
Colle Calzolaro bares its backside
to St Valentine's sun and me
to the steamy new ploughed panorama
and the far-flung stretching farms

And God in His Heaven but it's good to be
even a part in the sum of this
in this valley that spins about
in the temporary Winter heat
stung by the midday breeze that blows
from the furthest hills and snow –
curving purple shifting hills
whose folds of shadow emphasise
the sex and bush of far-off pines –
                    and it's good
to be walking again on St Valentine's map
heavy with light and Spring and blood

FIRE AND SNOW AND CARNEVALE

In winter fire is beautiful
beautiful like music
it lights the cave –
outside the people going home
drive slowly up the road – the strains
of phone-in Verdi on the radio
three hours back a fall of snow
sprinkled the furthest hill
where clouds have hung all winter

The day gets dark uneasy
dark and darker still
and you little son come home
riding the tail of the wind
in triumph – tall and almost ten
with confetti in your hair
home successful from the carnevale
with your two black swords
and your gold-handled knife

I feel the chill and hear
the absent sound of snow
when you come in –
white fantastic scorpions spit
in the fiery centre of the grate
plague pictures cauterised –
In winter fire is beautiful
and generous as music – may you
always come this safely home
in fire and snow and carnevale

MARCH IN DUBLIN – RETURN JOURNEY

At eleven o'clock
in the morning
that's how I found him
standing and gesturing
like a mad waiter –
and from his pockets
spoons knives and forks of words
flying in all directions

And on the floor
in the public bar
lying down in the middle of the room
his *compañero* roaring
in black leather trousers
toenails painted red
how he dare not go a-hunting
for fear of little men

And oh my friends
from that far country
I know what pains you took
to get here –
long long trains with buffet cars
years spent
in the holds of cattle boats
haunted nights in railway stations

IRISH SEED-POTATOES

1.

They won't grow there my neighbour said
in April – no foreign thing
will ever grow in the soil of Umbria

The Roman tried and we told him –
besides it is too early hereabouts
to think of planting seed-potatoes

And furthermore the moon is growing:
no seed will take
that is not planted in the shrinking moon

2.

At the start of May I pause a moment
in the cool after thunder
to admire their sharp-green stalks

Flourishing beside the vines – I am
thinking of Ireland and trying to return
to a message for my father

Begun when we came face to face
in the Achill house of Heinrich Böll
twelve months ago last March

Begun and lost in moving on from there –
to Dublin Moscow here
carrying these pages round

Repeating conversation with the past –
trying to keep perception bright
like putting sea-light under glass

3.

Until today I find myself at last
beside the corner of the tillage
reading Thomas Kinsella's anthology

Comforted by these few stalks
and recognising differences – somehow always
exiled stranger to my own

As if I had not served my time
sheltering in the clefts of rocks
on sodden hills where no sun shines

Coughing in foggy mail-boat mornings
labouring on foreign sites
and flying home at every chance

Enough to be here now and trying to write
a message for my wandering father
in whatever language fits –

Fits this and fits the journeying itself:
the starving freight of coffin-ships
and the wasting death of Goll Mac Morna

THE GOURMANDS OF EUROPE

Sometimes this year I see
the greed of Empire
here in the house and Burke and Hare
at large in the kitchen –
Arch Duke Rudolfo him
turned into a plant
turned green beyond osmosis

Turned into vegetable
fruit and cereal
those are grapes that were his eyes
red-faced from ingesting
he bobs among tomatoes
his forehead polished
to the texture of apples

Apricots corn and wheat
form the substance of his cheek
his ear a handsome mushroom
supports a bursting fig –
his jewels are passion-fruit
plums and raisins
hazel-nuts and nectarines

The Adam's apple is a pear
his furnace mouth
a full-fleshed chestnut
jumping from its spiky rind
brings air and pasta
to the bubbling lungs
of truffle oil and aubergines

He talks of food
throughout Affairs of State –
the rebel pepperoncino
sly mango wily marrow-flower
yams pulses peas courgettes –
all he has swallowed up
all he still hopes to eat

And God do I not sometimes long
to hear of something else?
To hear some news
of snipe or curlew
corn-crake cuckoo bittern thrush
or even maybe once to hear
of birds that sing in Berkeley Square

NOTES FROM THE COUNTRIES

I began to travel again. I travelled on a road till I got to a place where the road vanished into thin air. So I had to dream a road into existence. At the end of the road I saw a mirror. I looked into the mirror and nearly died of astonishment when I saw that I had turned white.
Azaro's father in "The Famished Road"
– Ben Okri

The first to awaken will be the Fish. Deep in the mirror we will perceive a very faint line and the colour of this line will be like no other colour. Later on, other shapes will begin to stir. Little by little they will differ from us; little by little they will not imitate us. They will break through the barriers of glass or metal and this time they will not be defeated... Others believe that in advance of the invasion we will hear from the depths of mirrors the clatter of weapons.
– Jorge Luis Borges, "The Book of Imaginary Beings"

1.

Nothing cleans the ground
said the Padrone of the Villa Ernestina
that evening above Pesaro – nothing cleans
the ground but planting *erba medica*:
and nothing clears the mind say I
but moving on: putting the wheels
in gear and moving on

And coming down at last
in sun and thunder from the Appenines
with our share of chest-pains
and the engine full of air
that's how we came to be here
oil blowing-out the dipstick
leaving a trail of thinning tar
that petered out in heat in Novilara
and that's how we come to be here
in the functional shade at noon
beneath the mediaeval tower
built by this man's father's father
to give a prospect of the sea –
Stranger than the Cyclops eye
of Military Intelligence
in Crossmaglen
Improbable as San Gimigniano

And what did we ever claim to be
in all our caravanserei
run so ragged on our journeys
climbing up to all these hill-towns
but *seme di pioppi* – poplar seeds
that drift across the valleys
bell-sounds on the necks of horses
on treeless plains above the timber line –

people of the high fields
travellers of the wandering rocks
with tongs and cauldron?
Who did we ever claim to be
but the stories we carry with us –
half of the cake with my blessing
or the whole of the cake with my curse

And happening here by chance at last
without the benefit of clock or compass
was nothing more
than falling into Prospero's garden
familiar recognised surprises
like hearing the whistle blow
on the far off cars of the night-train
for real for the first time
when I woke for a moment
turning in sleep in Milford
Michigan – or here today
among pines and palms and wild asparagus
watching the ships below
tacking along the wind to Venice
remembering the letters of Aretino
where murder and money and dust are real
as chance encounters in the street
or revisiting the Magic Mountain
climbing up again through
shaky mornings in the Rif
or standing in a wind-scrubbed square
in shock at evening in Urbino
dazed by the light beneath the walls
of the Dukes of Monte Feltro
and hoping to go home again
to settle into stone-flagged kitchens
to be welcomed into conversation
in houses that are gone –
To be going home like Marco Polo
To be going home like Carolan

74

2.

Memory is a heavy coat
worn sometimes back to front
against the rain: I see
my mother's father on an open road
dead before I was born

Walking a hundred years ago
and wonder if I've dressed him right
in hard-hat frieze-coat
waist-coat watch and chain
walking homeward from the town

Against the wind and rain-
washed countryside of Land Disputes
eviction emigration – the world outside
the walled-in trees and deep
solidified demesnes of Meath

He stayed when others left
for Melbourne Perth and San Francisco
leaving me a place unoccupied
a track worn down across the fields
a photograph I shelter from the light

Some little roads with weary ghosts
a well that might run dry
broken china in the garden
a settle-bed that's long since empty
all the ticking turned to dust –

Memories of childhood –
pink roses on the kitchen delph
and that's how frail we are
too quick to anger – so defenceless
in our seasons and so easy to break up

3.

Even without the nightingales
these women in the summer garden
of Augusta's house
Augusta Giorgia Mariamne
make up the persons of a Tragic play
while in the wings
a tableau from a photograph
five others dressed in crinolines
provide a chorus tint of sepia
gathered timeless at the gate
waiting for the messenger –
the dogs are sleeping in the shade
each symbol in its place
and every boy of ten
in leather sandals
could be Orestes or Telemachus

There are no mirrors here
except the hazy random sea
no lake of metal open to the sky
breaks up the pattern of the hills
and clouds and mountains to the south –
Fulvio – ten – is Giorgia's son
incumbent of the cryptic paths
those half-reclaimed and those
whose marble stones sink further down
into the earth – the Queen
his mother dark and Greek
a traveller from a curving vase
whipped from the House of Atreus
and brought here from Cattolica –
a movement of matt wax at night
and dressed in black
she glides among the trees and tables

Once more the King is missing
from the picture – gone to Thebes
Protector of The Buttock-Fields
on one of the beaches far below
his waking hours are passed
in the muster stretch and catch of thongs
about the legs and crotch –
here the humming garden sings
throughout the afternoon
and every boy of ten
becomes in turn Ajax or Achilles –
another sighting of the Fleece
beyond the Adriatic
some further news of Thrace
a severed head falls from a tree
wrapped up in leaves and dill
a figure hanging from a butcher's hook
and another piece of shrapnel
comes bursting from the lamp

4.

The mythologies that families weave
to hold themselves together –
Your house has burned down
and *You've* no home to go to
my one-legged uncle's nautical academy
shelled by mistake by the *Helga*

Crossed legends
of the great cook and the heroic drinker
or the alcoholic painter
whose fingers never shook
I had a message here today
a slogan on a cup – it read:
the geography of yearning

Lily Dunne in her apron strings in Dublin
walking around the snug
on wires like a crab in the sun
oh the nerves missus
the nerves oh the nerves missus
the nerves the nerves the nerves

And did the drowned man
have his arms across his chest in resignation
or was he fighting still for air?

And what of me – sitting here
in this conservatory
waiting for the wind to hit
the hanging chimes again
and reading over-and-over the legend
of Blood Fish and Bone

5.

This was the summer of the year I hoped
to open out the rann
to reach the place beyond mythologies

To see the monsters all unmasked
moving further into age
where one can make admissions without guilt

The summer of the year I built
my four-square shelter in among the trees
beneath some oaks upon a terraced hill

The year I tied back thorns
and cut away the undergrowth
to make a gap for sunlight to come through

And this was my retreat – five upright
posts of heavy chestnut
the roof was reed-canes from the lake

Laid on rafters from a ruined house –
for furniture a table chair
and hammock for the evening sun

And like an aging Satyr gone to seed
among the trees
half visible against the light on leaves

I came to be acquainted with the wood
crab-apples falling on my roof
small creatures dropping from the oaks

The daily flight-path of the clouds
drifting over from the lake
and all the noise and uproar

Along the forest floor – the slow
smooth rustle of a snake
sliding up against the bank

Quick crash of lizards
through the brittle crust – the
sudden cries of goats alarms of birds

Flying ants and stinging flies
and children's voices on the breeze
came with the drifting poplar seeds

This was the summer of the year
that Niall learned Italian
and learned to beat the video games

In Carlo's pizzeria –
took up karate fell in love
and all the other rites of passage

Appropriate at ten – the year
the post-colonialists arrived
to turn us into Tunbridge Wells

And this was our retreat –
forced out and on the road again
in flight we gave up argument

Seeing who the monsters were –
in argument we can persuade ourselves
that we are surer than we are

6.

What a way to present yourself
said the Doctor
when I got the clapped-out
twenty hundredweight van to Dublin
against the odds –
what a way to present yourself
he repeated
looking down from the fourth
floor of his script
lifting his shoulders and lighting
a Freudian cheroot

Did he think I'd been rehearsing
all the road up from the South?

But that fish this morning
on the lake
breaking the under-surface of the mist –
does a fish present itself
when it leaps?
That dead bird
beneath the Church at Aghabog –
or that long-shadowed walker
that struts beneath my window?

And am I not always listening
over the noise of the engine
for other voices –
other invitations home?
Are you lost are you lost – and
how should I know till I get there?

Did you meet anyone on the road?
I did
And did they ask you anything?
Yes they did
And what did you tell them?
Nothing! Nothing! I told them nothing!
Told them nothing? Good!

7.

What was going on there when the light
became so bad I couldn't see
what we were eating? I was preoccupied

About how carelessly those people came
from Iron Cross or Tunbridge Wells
and thinking of Ó Bruadair

Is mairg nach fuil 'na dhubhthuata,
cé holc duine 'na thuata,
ionnás go mbeinn mágcuarda

Idir na daoinibh duarca: Into
the second week of June – I wrote –
and all the bright days pass

But not with any record of their going –
our sceptered islanders are back
in occupation – landed wearing GB plates

With Marks and Spencer bags
a weekly pre-paid order for The Telegraph
and sacks of charcoal Packed In England

Our super-market pilgrims
have turned us into playtime once again
and little since is actual – they

Spend a half hour at the flower-bed
every morning – an outing to the shops
at ten o'clock

Then home preparing lunch
with glass in hand – and when we eat
before we do the clearing up

The making of the next meal has begun
until one day of incidental sun
becomes another and now May itself is gone

A haze of Sunday Supplement observances –
outdoor cooking tasting wine
amusement at the quaintness of the neighbours

Unable to speak normally to children
but lavishing affection on the cat –
and yet you say they're decent people

For all the drinking and the greed
they don't give in to sweat or indolence
are not consumed by alcohol or guilt

Just killing time with tedium
and pouring good days after bad – eating
drinking filling empty bottles up

And looking sad-eyed at the world
till all our waking hours begin
to seem like sleeping with the enemy

And here the enemy is weariness –
The weariness I always felt
each time I passed through Crewe going South

That undirected rage and puzzlement –
there's some agenda here
I cannot get a grip of – some arrogance

That keeps them safely from the edge –
among the blood-red flowers I note
the icons of our histories

Colonial and colonised:
the stuff of pomp and circumstance
angels of an iron age

Plantation symbiosis

8.

Today the day after rain
in recollection
I am listening
to the new-washed sounds of birds
trying out the air again
and thinking – this misdirected anger
ill-becomes me

Given sanctuary we all should be
as generous as birds –
like deer upon the avenue at night

lift up the rann
rise up the air and open it out

But this is not a fairy-tale
and did you know that I had met
a witch here once –
a vampire child with a machine gun
who blew everyone away?
Who set out to show me
we own nothing
least of all time and space

But what else have we got –
what have we got if not
space and history
and the stories we carry with us

I have a store of baggage too
rise up the air and open it out

Did I not tell you that I met
a witch here once?
A white-haired woman
in a long black coat
nodding and dancing among the trees –
who set out to show me
we own nothing
least of all time or space

not time or space
or nakedness
not even owning the air we breathe
owning nothing

Having no control over others
not smiles or whispers
or night-time quickness of breath
not even an instant shared
we own nothing
    neither ourselves
    nor touch
nor the momentary sounds of birds

and that was the bleakest of times
rise up the air and open it out

And in this day – is this the day
some Sunday maybe
is this the day it starts?
So hard to tell where histories begin –
when some cell thinks
to go askew within the blood –

Or that figure
nodding and dancing on the hill up there
among the trees?
    Or only a wayward bush?

9.

So what kind of dualist are you? Barnet
agus Beecher Hedges *agus* Stowe
were somehow there at the start of it –

I remember the winter of 'forty-seven
rattling home from school on the tram
getting off at Holles Street

And peeing in the snow in Merrion Square
being five and sick and seeing
gigantic firelit aunts around my bed

Later when I was seven and well
I ran down a hill to my grandmother's house
through flying heavy country snow

The hunched green bus to Granard brought me
past humps of turf in the Phoenix Park –
turf we set to dry in the oven –

Staggering on through Dunboyne and Trim
past Walker's Georgian house and lands
and Parr's and Alley's and the Hill of Ward

Into Athboy and the dung-soiled street
to drop me down at Nugent's corner –
and I walked out of town on the empty road

Past the graveyard and up the hill
through hills themselves beyond horizons –
to the hens that clucked in the yard

To my grandmother's fire and glass of port
and salty bacon on a chimney-hook –
to the fire where she aired her shrouds

And the daily prayers she offered up
for the canonization of Oliver Plunkett
and three days' warning of death –

And whatever else might chance to pass
in our weather-soaked world – ghosts walked
along the roads at night

Cries of vixens echoed in the dark
with news of neighbours' loss
or accidents that happened in Australia

While round and round and round in Dublin
thirty children in a circle
sang and marched about the room

York Road Dun Laoghaire 1947
and an autocratic hand beat time on a piano
How many kinds of wild-flowers grow

In an English Country Garden
I'll tell you some of the names that I know
and the rest will surely pardon

Also victims of paralysis and Empire
Kingstown Grammar they called the school
at the end of the Free-State tram

That brought us daily to Dun Laoghaire
and I read the Bible and Death of Nelson
with Armstrong Ireland Goodman Devlin

Goodbody Draper Gentleman Long
and my mother worked to teach us Gaelic
Republican and pluralist

Cumann na mBan with the same beliefs
that sixty troubled years ago
cost her a teaching post in Dundalk –

Today in Monaghan and looking down
from this Big House upon the lake and garden
gauging the familiar rain

The turning of the season and the leaves
with my own fifty years between
it seems appropriate and almost unimportant

Except that all the women I have known
were singular – my mother and her mother
and all the women who have worked these hills

Were singular and real:
I think of the *vicina* in the white house
across the road in Umbria

The way she walks on broken ground –
through geese and clamps and binder-twine
as self-contained about her business

As sure of hammer sickle scythe

10.

We have been
living with strangers
our partners in this house who said –
the Irish? I mean even so and if
we gave the Irish their freedom now
they wouldn't know
what to do with it ... would they?
Would they? They wouldn't
know what to do with it

Does nothing change
and how often do we have to see
this same boorish scene repeated
this manic arrogance?
Hard-money heroes coming-on
like Superman in Moscow
and Audie Murphy always
striding through Saigon –

And we continue trying to avoid
some half-cocked confrontation
with the grievance that is history
polite and liberal and angry –
but the truth is
I was almost driven mad by rage
anger at brutality in uniform
and out of it
at shootings at Loughgall
bombings in Warrington
at murder in the streets
angry for the dispossessed
and the homeless on the Underground
angry with complacency
and the pietistic rule of law and order

Angry at jejune Revisionists
as at ill-informed intransigence
at good poetry in bad translation
angry with committee-men
calling in on self-promotion
angry with sleeveens
obsequious and reverential
at funerals the morning after
when embarrassments have been
disposed of decently
and safely laid to rest

Angry with the grunt and
duck-billed platitude
that telegraph the Tory message
and all lick-spittle merchants
touters of received opinions
and Received Pronunciations
angry at over-simplifiers
canting boors and bully-boys
and anyone who takes
common human courtesy for weakness

And I am angry still
angry with myself
for being there at all
angry with myself for keeping silent
angry with my memories
of taking to the hills
angry with myself
for wasting time in folly
angry with myself in truth –
and this is folly too
angry pointlessly with you
for not being someone else

11.

Where did you go dead fathers
we send out letters no-one answers

Niall son we are I think
          mad parachutists
dropping through a tiny patch of sky
and landing nowhere –
that's who we are
people of the Ice Queen
the sunset
and the Hag of Beare
that's what we have become

where did you go dead fathers
out past the morning ships
leaving me here on the shore

When I was twelve or so
in Blackrock Baths
a naked man attacked me once
he spat and said – you
you're cultured Irish
you play the harp...

What hidden businesses
were going on there?
What contorted angers
hatred and disgust?

where are you gone dead fathers
who walked on empty Sunday paths

Oh child I wish that I did –
and if only he knew the half of it
where are you now dead fathers
who understood music and numbers

This time last year
standing in the dark in Moscow airport
at the baggage carousel
I met a woman in a stetson
an urgent messenger from home
who said –

    You know? In the madhouse
the general opinion was – and
this they consoled themselves with –
that whatever about the rest
there was one –
there was one who hadn't a hope
in hell
    not a hope in hell
not a hope not one
of coming through –
        and that was you

where did you go dead fathers
who understood poetry – life without hope
or did she think I hadn't noticed?

Son did I tell you
one time I was happiest?
In the Krassikov's orchard
out past Tchekova
digging a hole in the Russian earth

turning over the Russian earth
without thought
                just that
digging a hole for rotten apples
digging a hole among the birches

12.

When will we set out again
to look for Craggenaughan?
Or can such sudden
rightness be repeated?

To be going home like Marco Polo
Coming home like Carolan

That red leaf
on the steps of the big stone House
such a sudden splash
of scarlet –
the outline of a snow-flake
starfish and anchor

The crystals call us back
and the leaves
that fall into our rooms at night

But call us back to what – to sit
at the foot of the stairs
in the hall composing
farewells to music and to poetry?

And we come back from wandering
to find ourselves foreign
foreign to the streets of childhood
new buildings fill the gaps
in memory – new voices words and accents
occupy our thoughts

Children grow that much bigger
that much older
in this Republic of the Mind
we carry with us
there is no preventing
new alliances of monsters
the idiot jeers that echo
from the school-yard
or the terrible simpering faces
of people who were young with us

You find that you have
spent your life
fighting with monsters
arguing one agenda
discussing one set of problems
sorting out one situation
until all-and-nothing changes

Not easy to be fluid
as Ivan Malinovski was
as I saw him here
in front of the fire
on Selskar Terrace
untouched and strange
in knee-length britches
speaking Critiques for Himself –
and even if one were
we don't have another lifetime
for a second run at it

Maybe that's why the
Jesuit student of metaphysics
hoping for poetry
made all his notes in prose
a mistake a mistake

With one chance only
to hit the plateau of desire
I can go back in time
and just for now –

Stopped on suspicion
by the police in New Ross
Washed away by the rain
before welcome in West Cork
Best of MacElligott's
welcomes in Kerry
Warmth and shelter in Kilkee
before the sea froze over
Stung by the wind
above Loop Head – now
your grandson sits beside me
as we drive the empty
road for Ennis
drinking Seven Up
eating a pizza –
and what are we doing
but looking
looking for the country
where we are not foreign

rolling in the Van
with the windows open
and together
we're searching for Craggenaughan